Mother's Memories

For my Daughter

God could not be everywhere and therefore he made mothers.

PROVERB

...daughters are the thing.

J.M. BARRIE

Mother's Memories
For my Daughter

WRITTEN AND COMPILED BY DEBORAH NIXON

DESIGNED AND PHOTOGRAPHED BY ROBYN LATIMER

LANSDOWNE

For Lucille

Published by Lansdowne Publishing Pty Ltd
Level 1, 18 Argyle Street, The Rocks, Sydney NSW 2000, Australia

First published 1997
Reprinted 1998, 1999, 2000

© Copyright Lansdowne Publishing Pty Ltd 1997

ISBN 1 86302 590 1

Cover Photograph: George Kamper, The Photo Library of Australia
Printed in Singapore by Tien Wah Press (Pte) Ltd

To: ....

With love from:

....

CONTENTS

WHY THIS BOOK IS FOR YOU, MY DAUGHTER

....

....

....

....

... the relationship of mother and child
remains indelible and indescribable ...
the strongest bond upon this earth.

THEODOR REIK

"That moment", the King went on,
"I shall never, never forget!"
"You will, though, "the Queen said,
"unless you make a memorandum of it."

LEWIS CARROLL

A little about me, your mother...

My Names ....
....

Birthdate ....
....

Birthplace ....
....

Star sign ....
....
....

so that you may know me

[P H O T O G R A P H]

"Who was your mother?" "Never had none!"said the child, with another grin.
"Never had any mother? What do you mean? Where were you born?"
"Never was born!" persisted Topsy.

HARRIET BEECHER STOWE

YOUR FAMILY TREE

YOUR MOTHER

Names

....

YOUR
GRANDMOTHER

Names

....

Birthdate

....

Birthplace

....

Birthdate

....

Birthplace

....

YOUR
GRANDFATHER

Names

....

Birthdate

....

Birthplace

....

Your Grandmother's
Mother

....

....

Your Grandmother's
Father

....

....

Your Grandfather's
Father

....

....

Your Grandfather's
Mother

....

....

Your Grandmother's
Grandmother

....

....

Your Grandmother's
Grandfather

....

....

Your Grandfather's
Grandfather

....

....

Your Grandfather's
Grandmother

....

....

YOUR FAMILY TREE

YOUR FATHER
Names

....
Birthdate

....
Birthplace

....

YOUR
GRANDMOTHER
Names

....
Birthdate

....
Birthplace

....

YOUR
GRANDFATHER
Names

....
Birthdate

....
Birthplace

....

Your Grandmother's
Mother

Your Grandmother's
Father

Your Grandfather's
Father

Your Grandfather's
Mother

Your Grandmother's
Grandmother

Your Grandmother's
Grandfather

Your Grandfather's
Grandfather

Your Grandfather's
Grandmother

Memories of my mother and father
(your grandmother and grandfather)

....

....

....

....

....

What you called your grandmother and grandfather

....

....

"What do girls do who haven't any mothers to help them through their troubles"?

LOUISA MAY ALCOTT

Memories of my grandparents
and other special people in my life

...The trees in the street are old trees used to living with people,
Family trees that remember your grandfather's name.

STEPHEN VINCENT BENET

FAMILY PICTURES

[PHOTOGRAPH]

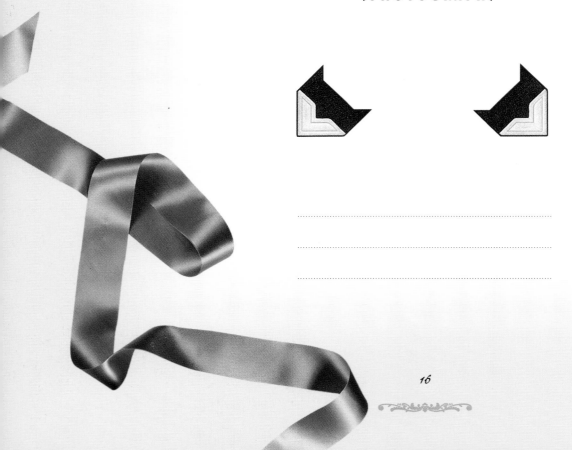

....

....

....

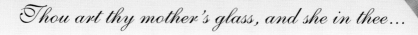

Thou art thy mother's glass, and she in thee...

WILLIAM SHAKESPEARE

[PHOTOGRAPH]

....

....

....

My beginnings

My earliest memory

....

....

....

....

....

Where I grew up

....

....

....

....

....

18

WHEN I WAS A GIRL

My best recollections of childhood

....

....

....

....

....

Books and other things I loved

....

....

....

....

....

PHOTOGRAPHS

[PHOTOGRAPH]

[PHOTOGRAPH]

....

....

....

MY SCHOOL DAYS

My first school ....

....

My first school friend ....

....

How I got to school ....

....

Glimpses into how it was then ....

....

....

....

[PHOTOGRAPH]

[PHOTOGRAPH]

24

PLAYTIME THEN

My favorite toy ....

....

My favorite doll ....

....

My dreams ....

....

My friends ....

....

Games and schemes I remember ....

....

....

25

WHERE I LIVED

My house

[PHOTOGRAPH]

My room

What I remember most about my room when I was young

....

....

....

....

....

More memories of my childhood

....

....

....

....

PETS

[PHOTOGRAPH]

Pets' names ....

....

....

[PHOTOGRAPH]

Pets' names ....

....

....

My teenage years

A teenage daughter is easier to love in retrospect.

JAN DU PLESSIS

Boys

Falling in love

....

....

....

....

What I learnt that I would like to tell you

....

....

....

....

MILESTONES IN MY LIFE

My first trip ....
....
....

My first kiss ....
....
....

My first job ....
....
....

The first time I bought something for myself ....
....
....

My first car ....

....

Other firsts ....

....

....

Memorable foods ....

....

....

Unforgettable experiences ....

....

....

Formative influences in my life ....

....

....

STORIES FROM MY LIFE

As a young woman

....

....

....

....

....

[PHOTOGRAPH]

How life was then

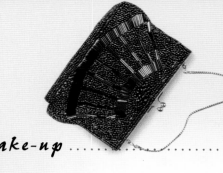

The fashions

Make-up ....

....

Hair ....

....

Clothes ....

....

Shoes ....

....

Some of my favorite things

....

....

....

....

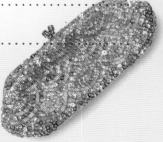

WHAT I HAVE ACHIEVED IN MY LIFE

FOND MEMORIES
AND SPECIAL MOMENTS

WHEN I MET YOUR FATHER

[PHOTOGRAPH]

The special things about your father

What attracted me to him

....

....

Recollections of our years together

....

....

....

....

Our first thoughts of you

....

....

....

OUR WEDDING

Date

....

Time

....

Place

....

[P H O T O G R A P H]

PHOTOGRAPHS

[PHOTOGRAPH]

WHEN I FOUND OUT ABOUT YOU

....

....

....

....

....

....

....

....

Evening star, you bring all things which the bright dawn has scattered:
you bring the sheep, you bring the goat, you bring the child back to its mother.

SAPPHO

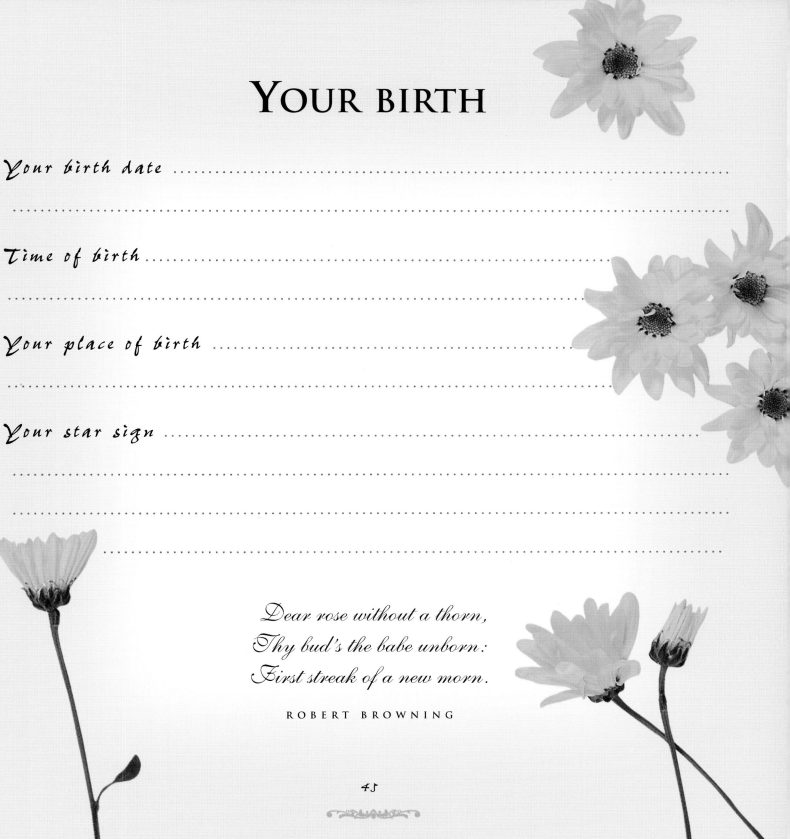

YOUR BIRTH

Your birth date ....

....

Time of birth ....

....

Your place of birth ....

....

Your star sign ....

....

....

Dear rose without a thorn,
Thy bud's the babe unborn:
First streak of a new morn.

ROBERT BROWNING

YOUR NAME

Your names ....

What your names mean ....

....

....

Why we chose your names ....

....

....

When mother love makes all things bright,
When joy comes with the morning light,
When children gather round their tree,
Thou Christmas Babe, we sing of thee!

TUDOR JENKS

What you might have been called

· ·

· ·

· ·

· ·

What everyone said about you

· ·

· ·

· ·

· ·

· ·

What you looked like as a baby

[P H O T O G R A P H S]

FIRST DAYS WITH YOU

. . . .

. . . .

. . . .

. . . .

. . . .

. . . .

Say, what is the spell, when her fledglings are cheeping,

That lures the bird home to her nest?

Or wakes the tired mother whose infant is weeping,

To cuddle and croon it to rest?

...For I'm sure it is nothing but Love!

LEWIS CARROLL

49

PHOTOGRAPHS

[PHOTOGRAPH]

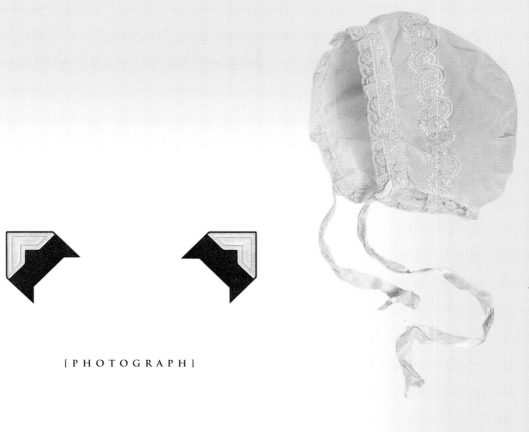

[PHOTOGRAPH]

A babe in the house is a well-spring of pleasure.

MARTIN F. TUPPER

My thoughts when you came into my life

....

....

....

....

....

Each mother's nurturing breast
Feeds a flower of bliss,
Beyond all blessing blest

ALGERNON CHARLES SWINBURNE

Of all the joys that brighten suffering earth,
What joy is welcom'd like a newborn child!

CAROLINE NORTON

The first time you . . .

Your first smile ....

The first time you sat up ....

The first time you crawled ....

The first time you walked ....

Baby darling, wake and see,
Morning's here, my little rose;
Open eyes and smile at me
Ere I clasp and kiss you close.
Baby darling, smile! For then
Mother sees the sun again

EDITH NESBIT

53

WALKING AND TALKING

[P H O T O G R A P H]

Your first steps ....

....

Your first words ....

....

Special phrases ....

....

EATING

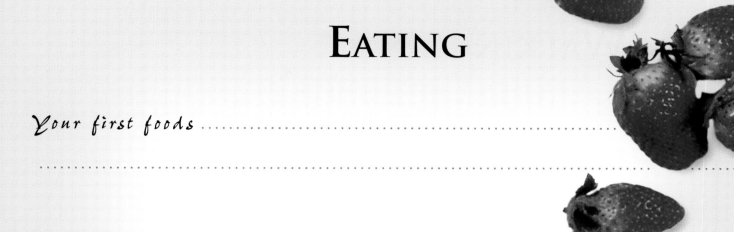

Your first foods ....

....

Your favorite foods ....

....

....

....

[PHOTOGRAPH]

♫

SLEEPING

How you slept ....

....

....

....

....

....

Sweet dreams form a shade
O'er my lovely infant's head
Sweet dreams of pleasant streams
By happy silent moony beams.

WILLIAM BLAKE

Oh hush thee, my babie, thy sire was a knight,
Thy mother a lady, both lovely and bright.

SIR WALTER SCOTT

LULLABIES

Fais do do, ma petite fille
Fais do do, t'auras du lo lo
Maman est en haute, qui fait des gâteaux
Papa est en bas, qui fait du chocolat
Fais do do, ma petite fille
Fais do do, t'auras du lo lo.

Hush, little baby don't say a word,
Mama's gonna buy you a mocking bird.
If that mocking bird don't sing,
Papa's gonna buy you a diamond ring.
If that ring is made of brass,
Mama's gonna buy you a looking glass.
If that looking glass gets broke,
Papa's gonna buy you a billy goat.
If that billy goat don't pull,
Mama's gonna buy you a cart and bull.
If that cart and bull turn over,
Papa's gonna buy you a dog named Rover.
If that dog named Rover don't bark,
Mama's gonna buy you a horse and cart.
If that horse and cart fall down,
You'll be the sweetest little baby in town!

SONGS YOU LOVED TO SING

Music you enjoyed

Twinkle twinkle, little star
How I wonder what you are.
Up above the world so high
Like a diamond in the sky.
Twinkle twinkle, little star
How I wonder what you are.

Baa Baa Black Sheep, have you any wool?
Yes Sir. Yes Sir. Three bags full.
One for the master. One for the dame.
And one for the little girl who lives down the lane.

YOUR BEST-LOVED BOOKS

....

....

....

....

....

Other favorite things

....

....

*Learn to read slow: all other graces
Will follow in their proper places.*

WILLIAM WALKER

As a little girl

Your early years

....

....

....

....

Dear Mamma, if you just could be
A tiny little girl like me,
And I your mamma, you would see
How nice I'd be to you.
I'd always let you have your way;
I'd never frown at you and say,
"You are behaving ill today,
Such conduct will not do".

SYDNEY DAYRE

DAYS AT HOME

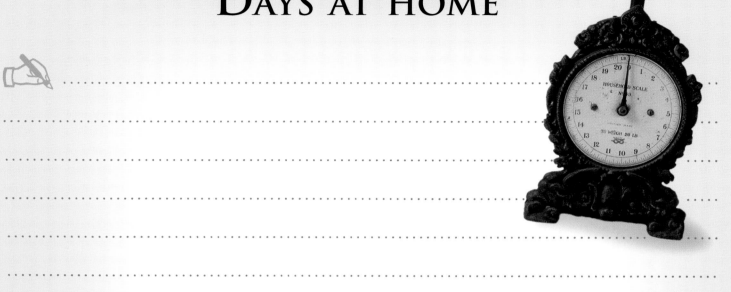

. . . .

. . . .

. . . .

. . . .

. . . .

What is home without a mother?

ALICE HAWTHORNE

They say there is no other
Can take the place of mother.

GEORGE BERNARD SHAW

Things we enjoyed doing together

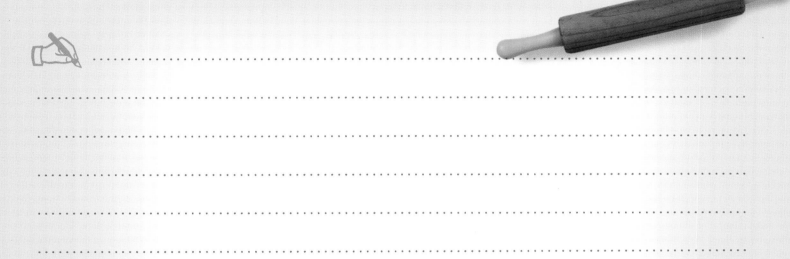

[PHOTOGRAPH]

Your favorite games

YOUR FAVORITE THINGS

Toys ....

....

....

....

Dolls ....

....

....

....

Pastimes ....

....

....

....

YOUR FIRST DAY AT SCHOOL

....

....

....

....

....

....

Your teacher's name ....

....

Your best friends ....

....

....

YOUR SCHOOL DAYS

....

....

....

....

....

....

Clubs and activities after school

....

....

....

....

....

GROWING UP

WHEN YOU WERE A TEENAGER

....

....

....

....

....

....

....

....

....

....

....

PHOTOGRAPHS AND CLIPPINGS

[PHOTOGRAPH]

From your childhood

[PHOTOGRAPH]

How special you are to me

....

....

....

....

....

I have a small daughter called Cleis,
who is like a golden flower
I would not take all Croesus' kingdom
with love thrown in, for her.

SAPPHO

How life has changed for me since you came along

....
....
....
....
....
....

Love still has something of the sea
From whence his mother rose

SIR CHARLES SEDLEY

A dreary place would this earth be
Were there no little people in it;
The song of life would lose its mirth,
Were there no children to begin it.

J.G. WHITTIER

SPECIAL TIMES WITH YOU

The world has no such flowers in any land
And no such pearl in any gulf the sea
As any babe on any mother's knee.

ALGERNON CHARES SWINBURNE

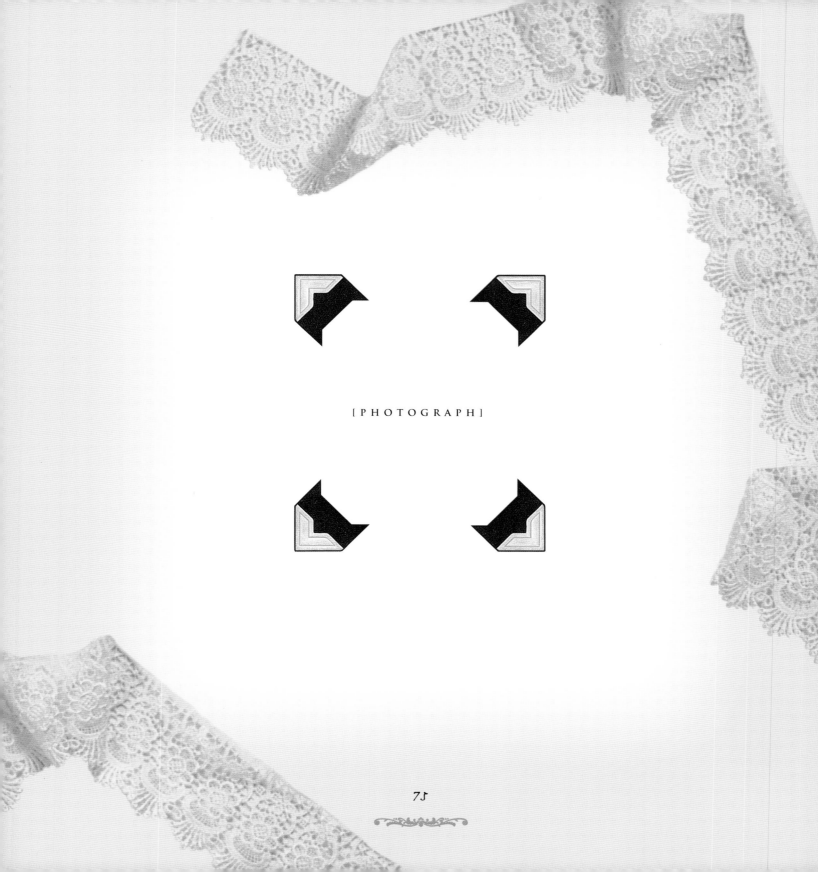

[PHOTOGRAPH]

WISE WORDS
FROM WISE WOMEN

Trust your gut.

BARBARA WALTERS

If you don't paddle your own canoe, you don't move.

KATHARINE HEPBURN

No one can make you feel inferior without your consent.

ELEANOR ROOSEVELT

It's never too late to be what you might have been.

GEORGE ELIOT

MOTHERLY SAYINGS

from mothers and grandmothers everywhere

If a thing is worth doing, it is worth doing well.

Begin somewhere; you cannot build a reputation on what you intend to do.

Genius is immediate, but talent takes time.

Just because everyone else is doing it, doesn't make it right.

Do unto others as you would have them do unto you.

Don't talk with your mouth full.

Wear clean underwear.

Carry enough money to telephone home.

Never start anything that you don't want to become a habit.

Keep your wits about you.

Sayings and advice from your mother and grandmother

....

....

....

Mother knows best.

EDNA FERBER

THE IMPORTANT THINGS
FOR YOU TO REMEMBER

....

....

....

....

Who ran to help me when I fell,
And would some pretty story tell,
Or kiss the place to make it well,
My mother.

ANN TAYLOR

"Remember" is always a magic word,
but especially when mother and daughter use it.

JESSAMYN WEST

WHAT I WISH FOR YOU

....

....

....

....

....

Remember there's no other
As dear, where'er you roam,
So don't forget your mother
And the dear old home!

ANDREW B. STERLING

... But a mother's love endures through all.

WASHINGTON IRVING

[PHOTOGRAPH]